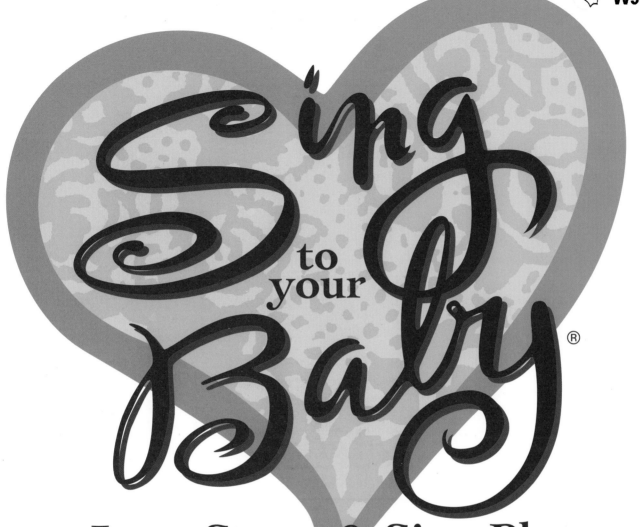

# Sing to your Baby

## Love Songs & Sing-Plays for New Families

### Book & Songs by Cathy Fink & Marcy Marxer

### Illustrations by James Nocito

www.singtoyourbaby.net

SONGSMITH
*an imprint of*
PETER E. RANDALL PUBLISHER
Portsmouth, New Hampshire
www.perpublisher.com

Community Music, Inc.
P.O. Box 461, Kensington, MD 20895

The text for the lyrics is set in Cochin Bold
All hand lettering created by James Nocito

For information about custom editions, special sales,
educational bulk sales, premium and corporate purchases
please contact info@singtoyourbaby.net

ISBN-978-0-9651036-5-7
Library of Congress Catalog Card Number:  2012900267

# Table of Contents

## Lyrics & Illustrations

# A Letter from
## *Sing To Your Baby*®
# Creators Cathy & Marcy

Dear Mom, Dad and Other Wonderful Folks Who Will be Singing to Your Baby,

As lifelong singers, songwriters and musicians, we have seen the power of music in the lives of children and their parents. Having a new little one in the house is a time of joy and wonder. Parents want to do everything they can to bond with their newborn and to strengthen that bond as their baby grows. One of the best ways to create a mutual bond is to *Sing To Your Baby*®.

In thousands of family concerts over more than 25 years, we have heard parents say, "I wish I could have sung to my baby, but..." - and for one reason or another they didn't. So, we have designed a program for all parents, grandparents and others in a new baby's circle of loved ones. With our help, you can hold your baby and sing away - by singing along with the CD. Singing can be an elemental communication tool that will last for years to come by using music together for fun, developing new skills and as an ongoing expression of love.

As we experimented with the project, we found expectant parents who wanted to start singing to their baby in the womb. There were siblings who sang to the baby along with Mom or Dad. Some adorably sang to their baby dolls while a parent sang to the baby. There are so many ways to use the simple concept of songs sung from the heart (and sometimes from the ticklebone).

Share with parents, grandparents, caregivers, aunts, uncles, siblings and godparents. And most importantly, take your time turning this into a daily activity. The rewards as you *Sing To Your Baby*® will last a lifetime.

Join us at www.singtoyourbaby.net. We'd love to hear from you, see pictures of you singing to your baby and keep you updated as we create new songs and activities.

*Cathy & Marcy*

## A NOTE ABOUT SINGING RANGES

Everyone's voice is unique, and women and men typically sing in different keys. So, we've recorded each song in two different keys. Though the "mom" keys are sung by a female voice and the "dad" keys are sung by a male voice, you should sing in whichever key is best for your voice. Each page will include a box containing the song or track numbers, along with the key in which each selection is sung, as the following example illustrates:

Track 1      Track 12
Mom-C        Dad-G

## SING TO ME! (from baby)

# i am your baby and i love your voice!

I don't care if you are a professional singer or even a good singer. Relax – I think you're a star! So let's not stress or criticize, let's just DO IT!

# let's find the time!

I know that you are busy – that's what being my Mom or Dad means. But you don't have to learn all the songs at once. Let's start by listening together. You will learn the lyrics in no time, but you can always use the book to help you.

# learn the lyrics anytime!

You can listen and learn the lyrics at times when we are apart: during your commute to or from work, while doing housework, while exercising, as you do errands, or at night when you want to unwind (this one you can do with me!).

4

# just you and me!

Consider listening on a portable listening device, in which you can put one ear bud in your ear (please be careful of volume) and still have one ear listening to me and my environment. Then I only hear YOU. I love hearing your voice.

# learn the songs before i arrive!

Start singing to me even before I am born, and then keep right on singing!

# i don't care if you know every word!

Just hum along with the songs and don't worry about lyrics. Your humming soothes and relaxes me. Use "la la la" instead of the words if that is more comfortable than humming – those of us with limited vocabularies enjoy "la la la".

# sing to me with or without the book!

You can easily read the lyrics while the book lies flat on a table or on the floor. Before you know it, you will be singing these songs to me without using the book or CD.

# my siblings can sing along too!

If I'm lucky enough to have siblings, they can sing to me along with you. They enjoy holding me and helping Mommy or Daddy. I would like to hear their voices, too!

# let's play along with the lyrics!

Singing IS playing, and being creative is part of the fun. You may come up with some special words that you want to sing to me. Make up your own words, just for us.

# put my name in the song!

Put my name in places where we sing the word "baby".
Instead of "Tickle little baby on the toe", you might sing
"Tickle little [my name] on the toe". Before long,
I'll start thinking, "That's me!"

# let's sing-play every day!

Once you become so comfortable with the songs
that you don't need the recording, just keep singing
to me. If you find that you're more comfortable
singing with the recording, no worries.

# let's socialize!

Let's get together with your friends and their
babies and sing together in the living room.
We can bond with our friends as we bond with
each other.

# Love Is What I Feel for You

Love is what I feel for you
Love is when I hold you too
Love fills me through and through
Love is what I feel for you

Peace is what I feel for you
Peace is when I hold you too
Peace fills me through and through
Peace is what I feel for you

Hope is what I feel for you
Hope is when I hold you too
Hope fills me through and through
Hope is what I feel for you

Joy is what I feel for you
Joy is when I hold you too
Joy fills me through and through
Joy is what I feel for you

Love is what I feel for you
Love is when I hold you too
Love fills me through and through
Love is what I feel for you

Track 1     Track 12
Mom-C     Dad-G

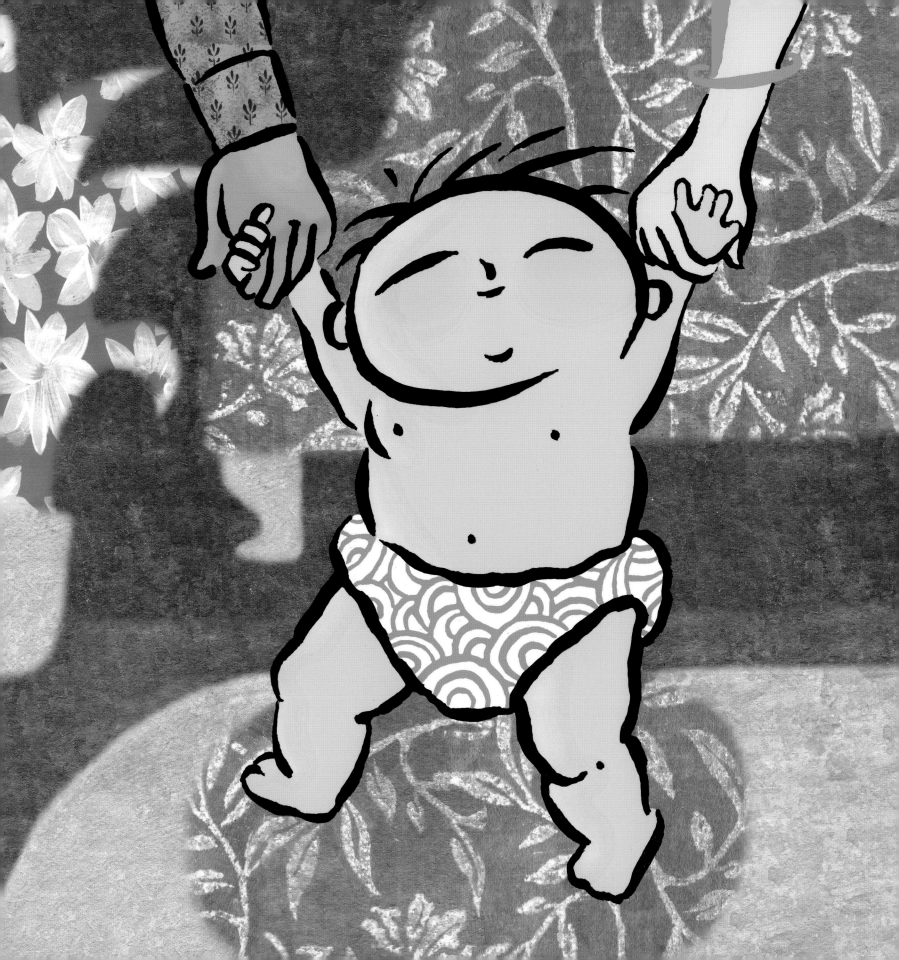

# Rockin' My Baby

1. Rockin' my baby in the morning
   Rockin' my baby in the afternoon
   Rockin' my baby in the morning
   Rockin' my baby take your worries away

2. Dancin' with my baby

3. Singin' with my baby

4. Doodlin' with my baby

5. Doodle doo'n doodle doo'n doodle doo ...

6. La la la la

7. Clappin' with my baby

8. Dancin' with my baby

9. Singin' with my baby

10. Rockin' my baby

11. Rockin' my baby

Track 2     Track 13
Mom-C      Dad-E

11

# Wake Up

Wake up my little baby, wake up
Wake up my little baby, wake up
Wake up my little sweetie pie, my little honey drop
Wake up my little baby, wake up

Kiss my little baby like this *(kiss)*
Kiss my little baby like this *(kiss)*
Kiss my little sweetie pie, my little honey drop
Kiss my little baby like this *(kiss)*

Rock my little baby, let's rock
Rock my little baby, let's rock
Rock my little sweetie pie, my little honey drop
Rock my little baby, let's rock

Tickle little baby, let's tickle *(tickle)*
Tickle little baby, let's tickle *(tickle)*
Tickle my little sweetie pie, my little honey drop
Tickle little baby, let's tickle *(tickle)*

Wake up my little baby, wake up
Wake up my little baby, wake up
Wake up my little sweetie pie, my little honey drop
Wake up my little baby, wake up

Track 3    Track 14
Mom-C    Dad-D

# Little Bitty Boat

Little bitty boat, rockin' on the water
Rockin' in the bright warm sun
Little bitty boat, rockin' on the water
Rockin' in the bright warm sun

*Refrain: Oh, oh, oh here we go again*
*Oh, oh rockin' in the bright warm sun*

Little bitty fish, swimmin' in the water
Swimmin' in the bright warm sun (2X)

*Refrain: Oh, oh, oh here we go again*
*Oh, oh swimmin' in the bright warm sun*

Little bitty shell, flippin' in the water
Flippin' in the bright warm sun (2X)

*Refrain: Oh, oh, oh here we go again*
*Oh, oh flippin' in the bright warm sun*

Little bitty wave, rollin' on the water
Rollin' in the bright warm sun (2X)

*Refrain: Oh, oh, oh here we go again*
*Oh, oh rollin' in the bright warm sun*
La La La…

Track 4     Track 15
Mom-F      Dad-G

# Chickadee

*Spoken*
Chicka-dee chicka-da chicka-doo chicka-do
Swingin' and singin', to and fro
Chicka-pee chicka-pa chicka-poo chicka-po
Chicka little baby gonna watch you grow

*Sung*
Chicka-dee chicka-da chicka-doo chicka-do
Swingin' and singin', to and fro
Chicka-pee chicka-pa chicka-poo chicka-po
Chicka little baby gonna watch you grow
Chicka little baby gonna watch you grow

Track 5     Track 16
Mom-C      Dad-E

# I Love You

La la la la la la la (3X)
La la la la
I love you

Mm mm mm mm mm mm mm (3X)
Mm mm mm mm
I love you

Oo oo oo oo oo oo oo (3X)
Oo oo oo oo
I love you

La la la la la la la (3X)
La la la la
I love you

Oo oo oo oo oo oo oo (3X)
Oo oo oo oo
I love you

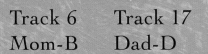

Track 6     Track 17
Mom-B       Dad-D

# Bouncing

*(carefully support your baby's head until baby can hold its own head up)*

Bouncing, bouncing
Baby on my knee
Bouncing, bouncing, 1-2-3!
(2X)
*(parent bounces baby on lap)*

Clapping, clapping
Baby on my knee
Clapping, clapping, 1-2-3!
(2X)
*(parent claps baby's hands)*

Tapping, tapping
Baby on my knee
Tapping, tapping, 1-2-3!
(2X)
*(tap baby's fingers to knee, tummy, shoulder...)*

Reaching, reaching
(2X)
*(baby and singer get a good stretch here)*

Hugging, hugging
(2X)
*(you know what to do!)*

Track 7       Track 18
Mom-C        Dad-A

# Baby's Got a Giggle

Baby's got a giggle, oh my
Baby's got a giggle, oh my
Baby's got a giggle, oh my
Tickle little baby on the toe

Tickle little baby on the knee

Tickle little baby on the tummy

Tickle little baby on the hand

Tickle little baby on the neck

Tickle little baby on the cheek

Tickle little baby on the ear

*Now we're gonna go backwards*
*(cheek, neck, hand, tummy, knee, toe)*

Track 8    Track 19
Mom-C     Dad-F

# Pretty Little Baby

Oh come to me my pretty
My pretty little bitty
My little bitty baby that I love

It's you that I adore more
And get down on the floor for
You're the one I sing my songs for
You're the one I'm thinking of

With your little hand in mine
We'll dance round the room
Hear that ukulele rhythm
Boom, boom, boom, boom

Oh, come to me my pretty
My pretty little bitty
My little bitty baby that I love

Track 9     Track 20
Mom-F     Dad-G

# Bye-Bye!

1. Bye-bye, bye-bye
   Waving bye-bye!
   Bye-bye, bye-bye
   Waving bye-bye!
   Fingers waving to our friends
   Let's wave bye-bye once again
   Bye-bye, bye-bye
   Waving bye-bye!

2. Blow a kiss, blow a kiss
   Blowing kisses!
   Blow a kiss, blow a kiss
   Blowing kisses!
   Blowing kisses to our friends
   Let's blow kisses once again
   Blow a kiss, blow a kiss
   Blowing kisses!

Track 10    Track 21
Mom-E       Dad-D

# Wherever You Go, I Love You

*Refrain: Wherever you go, whatever you do*
*Through all the changes you go through*
*I'll be there right next to you*
*I love you*

1. When you're too small to reach the sink
   So all you do is sit and think
   About how clean you would have been
   Know that I will love you then

*Refrain*

2. When you can button up your shirt
   And brush off your own dust and dirt
   When you can spell and write your name
   I will love you just the same

*Refrain*

3. When you lose your two front teeth
   And miss the things you used to eat
   And try to reach things up above
   I will give you all my love

*Refrain*

4. When you crawl into your bed
   And on a pillow lay your head
   When you're drifting off to sleep
   I will love you while you dream

*Refrain*

Track 11    Track 22
Mom-C      Dad-D

# *Sing To Your Baby*® - **Parent Guide**
**Laura G. Brown, Ph.D.**

*Sing to Your Baby*® presents simple songs that parents learn while singing along with the CD. Later you can sing independently to your child. This guide includes ideas as to how to best do this and how to "sing-play" to gain the most enjoyment from your singing time together. For more information on how your baby might respond to the songs, please visit **www.singtoyourbaby.net**.

## What is "sing-play"?

Singing is a type of creative play. Just imagine, if you pretend to be an animal as you sing a song about animals, you are engaging in creative play while singing. Also, as you personalize songs - by adding movements, special lyrics just for you and your child, or novel ways of singing them – you incorporate creativity.

Creative play and pretend play with a young child support social, emotional and intellectual development. Modeling this type of play, by sing-playing with your baby now, is a great first step in encouraging well-rounded development in the coming years.

## Why Sing To Your Baby?

Singing to your baby is just plain fun! In our fast-paced, goal-oriented society it is easy to forget how important it is to enjoy the journey. Perhaps the most important gift you can give both yourself and your baby is the time to relax and have fun as well as the consistent message that it is important to do so. We wish you and your baby many hours of joy singing together!

## Bonding

Bonding may be the most satisfying reason of all to sing to your baby. Bonding refers to the intense feelings that develop between parents and their baby. For some parents, those feelings are there the minute their child is born. For others, it takes time to develop those feelings. Either way, bonding is a process, and continues as both the child and the parent grow into the relationship. Bonding is essential to a child's well-being. The relationship between a parent and a child is the model upon which future relationships are based, so a strong bond can facilitate future relationships. Strong bonds also give the child a sense of security, self-identity and self-worth.

Parents don't have to "do" anything for bonding to occur. It evolves as they live with and care for their baby every day. But communicating love through close eye-to-eye communication, play and touch can help promote those feelings. Singing to your baby is an intimate way to accomplish this.

## Interest in Music

Singing to children helps promote an interest in music. Young children naturally want to be with their parents and to enjoy the things their parents do. So, if you make it clear that you love music by singing, your children may follow in your footsteps.

## Learning Skills

We are constantly learning more about how music exposure and instruction relates to learning skills. For example, rhythm and rhyme, prominent aspects of most songs, promote an awareness of the sounds within language that are related to pre-reading skills. We are not suggesting that singing to your baby alone will make your child good at math or reading. But it is a joyous way to foster your child's interest in music which may open the door to more beneficial music experiences as your child grows.

## Transitions

Babies and young children do better when there are routines and structure to their day. They feel safe when life is predictable. However, young children can have trouble ending a task they are enjoying (it's hard to stop playing to clean up before dinner). Songs are a great way to help children transition to the next activity. Singing the same good-night song every night teaches your baby that bedtime is approaching and that it is time to calm down. Similarly, an energetic clean-up song can help a toddler transition from play to clean-up mode seamlessly.

# Gratitude from CATHY & MARCY

We'd like to thank everyone who helped us in the creation of this project,
especially parents who gave us feedback
and encouragement over the past few years, including
Kim Garey, Joe Uehlein & Lane Windham,
Lisa Silverberg and Alisa Kaeser.
We also thank Betty Scott for inviting us to sing
to her new granddaughter, Chloe, in a circle of Chloe's loved ones.
We hope this will become a new tradition for new families.

## Thanks to the *Sing To Your Baby*® team:

**JAMES NOCITO -** Original Art and Graphics
**AMY C. WILLIAMS -** Book and CD Layout
**REGINA KELLAND -** Editing and Marketing
**ALISA KAESER -** All Things Organizational
and
**LAURA G. BROWN, Ph.D. -** Parents' Guide
**CARLETON KAESER -** Inspiration
**BEN HERSHMAN -** True Believer